How to Earn Passive Income with Crypto

Staking, Yield Farming, Lending, and DeFi Explained for Everyday Investors

By Joe Correa

Published by Live Stronger Faster

This book is for educational and informational purposes only. The author and publisher are not engaged in rendering legal, financial, or other professional advice. Readers should consult a qualified professional before making any financial decisions.

First Edition

Table of Contents

Introduction

For decades, the idea of earning passive income was limited to real estate, dividend stocks, or building a business. But the rise of cryptocurrency has opened up a revolutionary new world of decentralized finance—also known as DeFi—where anyone, anywhere, with just a phone and a crypto wallet, can earn money passively around the clock—even while sleeping. This financial transformation is unlike anything the traditional banking system has ever allowed. In this book, wc will explore how to harness this once-in-a-generation opportunity.

Welcome to *How to Earn Passive Income with Crypto*, Book 6 of the *Crypto Wealth Academy* series. This guide is for the everyday investor who wants to grow their crypto holdings without constantly buying and selling. Whether you're new to crypto or have some experience but haven't yet explored DeFi or passive yield opportunities, this book will show you practical, step-by-step strategies to start earning with minimal risk and effort.

Let's begin by clearing up a myth: earning passive income from crypto is not a get-rich-quick scheme. It's not about hype or speculative bets. Instead, it's about using proven financial tools—staking, lending, yield farming, and liquidity pools—through protocols that reward you for supporting blockchain infrastructure or providing capital to others. These opportunities mirror some traditional finance mechanisms, but in a decentralized, automated way that allows you to stay in control of your money.

You'll learn how staking works on proof-of-stake blockchains and which platforms offer the best returns. We'll demystify yield farming and explain why some people earn double-digit annual yields just by allocating tokens to decentralized exchanges. We'll cover crypto lending protocols like Aave and Compound, where you can lend stablecoins and earn consistent income—sometimes beating what banks pay in a year in just a month. And we'll walk you through risks such as impermanent loss, rug pulls, and smart contract vulnerabilities, so you don't fall into the common traps that many beginners face.

Unlike speculative crypto trading, passive income strategies focus on long-term growth and stability. They're ideal for people who want to accumulate crypto over time, diversify income streams, and take advantage of compound interest in a digital economy. You'll also hear about real-world case studies from people who started with as little as $100 and are now earning consistent monthly income from their holdings.

You don't need to be a tech expert to apply these strategies. This book is designed to simplify the technical terms, explain step-by-step processes, and provide beginner-friendly recommendations for wallets, networks, and platforms. We'll even guide you through setting up your first staking wallet, joining a lending pool, and tracking your earnings over time.

As we move into the coming years, DeFi will become an essential part of the global financial system. Those who understand how to navigate it today will be in the strongest position to build wealth tomorrow. Passive income from crypto is not only possible—it's happening right now, all over the world.

Let's dive in and unlock the tools, strategies, and platforms you can start using today to earn passive crypto income.

Chapter 1: Understanding Crypto Passive Income: The New Frontier of Wealth Building

In traditional finance, the term "passive income" typically evokes images of rental property checks, dividends from blue-chip stocks, or royalties from intellectual property. But the advent of blockchain technology and decentralized finance (DeFi) has introduced a new and potentially more accessible method of generating passive income—earning yield from crypto assets. This chapter lays the foundation for understanding how crypto enables financial systems that pay you not for hard labor, but for participating in decentralized ecosystems. Unlike volatile trading strategies that require market timing and constant screen-watching, crypto passive income involves setting up systems that work for you over time—accumulating value by providing security, liquidity, or lending capital in exchange for rewards.

The concept is simple: in the world of cryptocurrency, your money can work as an infrastructure provider. In a traditional bank, you deposit funds and the bank uses your money to make loans and earn profits—usually giving you a minimal return. In crypto, that same structure exists—but with a twist: the profits go back to you. You can earn for securing a blockchain network (staking), for offering liquidity on decentralized exchanges (yield farming or liquidity provision), or for allowing others to borrow your assets (lending protocols). Instead of centralized institutions being middlemen, smart contracts automatically handle the terms and distribute rewards. This innovation has allowed people all over the world, regardless of geographic or economic status, to begin building financial independence on a permissionless platform.

To start earning passive income in crypto, you must first understand the difference between **custodial** and **non-custodial** approaches. Custodial platforms, like Binance or Coinbase, offer staking and savings accounts with set interest rates—but you don't control the private keys, meaning the platform holds your funds on your behalf. Non-custodial methods, such as using a DeFi wallet like MetaMask or Trust Wallet with platforms like Aave or Lido, offer more control and often higher rewards—but come with higher risks and responsibilities. Your journey into passive income will depend on how much risk you're willing to take and whether you're ready to manage your own crypto wallets securely.

One of the most popular and beginner-friendly strategies is **staking**. Staking involves locking your crypto—usually in a Proof-of-Stake (PoS) network—in return for earning rewards.

These rewards are essentially interest paid for helping to validate transactions and maintain network security. Tokens like Ethereum (ETH), Cardano (ADA), and Polkadot (DOT) all offer staking. The yields can range from 3% to 15% annually, depending on network activity and demand. Some platforms allow you to stake with flexible terms, while others require you to lock up your tokens for a fixed period. The more decentralized route involves using self-hosted wallets or joining validator pools directly. While staking is relatively safe, the value of the token you're staking can fluctuate wildly—so it's important to consider both the yield and the underlying asset risk.

Next is **yield farming**, a more advanced but potentially higher-reward method of passive income. Yield farming involves providing liquidity to decentralized exchanges like Uniswap, PancakeSwap, or Curve. In simple terms, you lend your crypto into a pool that other traders can use to make swaps. In return, you earn transaction fees and often bonus tokens as rewards. The yield can be significant—ranging from 10% to 200% annually in some cases—but it's also accompanied by risks like **impermanent loss**, where the value of your staked tokens changes unfavorably due to price fluctuations, and **smart contract risk**, where bugs in the protocol could lead to loss of funds. For beginners, it's best to start small and with stablecoin pairs (e.g., USDC/DAI) to avoid the extreme volatility often seen in altcoin liquidity pools.

Another important avenue is **crypto lending**. Instead of offering your assets to exchanges for swaps, you lend them out directly to borrowers through decentralized lending platforms like Aave, Compound, or Venus. You earn interest, typically ranging from 2% to 12%, depending on the asset. This strategy is especially effective when using **stablecoins** like USDT, USDC, or DAI, which maintain their value and reduce the risk of price volatility. Lending is often safer than yield farming, especially when working with overcollateralized loans, meaning borrowers must lock up more crypto than they borrow. However, lending still requires you to be cautious of protocol stability and network congestion, both of which can affect your returns.

DeFi aggregators and **vaults** simplify passive income by automating these strategies. Platforms like Yearn.Finance and Beefy Finance automatically allocate your funds across the highest-yielding protocols, saving you from manually hunting for the best opportunities. They take a small fee but often produce higher net yields due to optimization strategies and auto-compounding. While convenient, this added layer of abstraction increases smart contract complexity—so only invest amounts you can afford to lose.

When comparing these strategies—staking, farming, and lending—it's important to consider your goals. If you want steady, low-risk returns, staking or stablecoin lending is a great place to begin. If you're looking for high yield and are comfortable with volatility and technical tools, farming or participating in vaults may suit you better. Most importantly, diversify your strategy across platforms and asset types. Never put all your funds into one protocol, especially one that's new, unaudited, or trending on social media for "unbelievable" returns.

Lastly, always calculate **real** yield—not just the token reward rate. A 50% APY might sound impressive, but if the token you're earning drops 90% in value, you've lost more than you gained. Use tools like DeFi Llama, Token Terminal, or APY.Vision to track actual return rates, risks, and historical performance. Always convert your expected yield into stablecoin or fiat equivalents to assess true profitability.

As we move forward in this book, each chapter will break down one of these major income strategies in full detail—how to set it up, what platforms to use, and how to protect yourself from loss. The goal isn't just to make you money, but to help you understand the architecture of DeFi so you can safely build wealth without constant involvement. Welcome to the frontier of modern financial freedom.

Daniel's Bitcoin story

Daniel had always played it safe with money. A modest savings account, a basic retirement fund, and a habit of clipping coupons—nothing fancy, but enough to feel secure. That all changed in 2021 when the pandemic rattled global markets and made him question the security he once believed in. His 401(k) took a hit, his savings lost purchasing power due to inflation, and the rising cost of living began outpacing his income. Daniel needed a new plan—one that didn't rely entirely on traditional finance. That's when he discovered the idea of earning passive income through cryptocurrency.

At first, Daniel was skeptical. He had heard about Bitcoin, sure, and even saw friends brag about big gains on social media. But he wasn't a gambler. He wasn't interested in chasing trends or timing the market. What intrigued him was something deeper: the concept of putting his crypto to work. He stumbled upon a video that explained staking and lending—not trading, but earning consistent income just by holding crypto assets. This felt different. It felt sustainable. He began to research in earnest.

Daniel's first foray was staking. He bought a small amount of Cardano (ADA) and transferred it to a mobile wallet. The idea of locking it in for rewards seemed risky at first, but the more he understood how Proof-of-Stake worked, the more confident he became. By delegating his tokens to a staking pool, he was helping secure the network and earning an annual percentage yield in return. It was slow, steady, and surprisingly easy to monitor. Every five days, he saw small amounts of ADA show up in his wallet—like clockwork. It wasn't much, but it was real. And it was his first taste of what passive crypto income could feel like.

Encouraged, Daniel moved on to DeFi lending. He converted some of his holdings into USDC, a stablecoin, and explored platforms like Aave and Compound. The process was technical at first—connecting MetaMask, navigating Ethereum gas fees, and understanding collateral ratios. But once the setup was complete, it was astonishingly smooth. Daniel deposited his USDC into a lending pool and watched his balance grow. The yield wasn't jaw-dropping—around 8% annually—but compared to his savings account back home paying 0.05%, it was revolutionary. More importantly, his risk was reduced thanks to the stable nature of USDC.

Still, curiosity got the better of him. Daniel kept reading about "yield farming" and saw stories of people earning double or triple-digit returns. He dipped a toe into this world by providing liquidity on PancakeSwap, choosing a stablecoin pair (USDC/DAI) to minimize volatility. In return, he received LP tokens and staked them on a yield aggregator. At one point, he was earning nearly 25% APY. But soon, Daniel learned about the darker side of DeFi. A protocol he considered using was hacked. A friend lost funds to a "rug pull." And Daniel himself experienced impermanent loss on another farming pair when one token price dropped dramatically. The lesson hit hard: high yield often comes with high risk.

Determined not to be deterred, Daniel adopted a more strategic approach. He diversified his passive income strategies—staking some assets, lending others, and only using battle-tested platforms with strong reputations and audits. He began calculating real APY, factoring in token value, platform fees, and gas costs. He also started using DeFi dashboards to track all his earnings in one place. Over time, what began as an experiment became a core pillar of his financial life. By the end of his first year, Daniel was earning several hundred dollars per month in passive income—enough to pay a few bills or reinvest into more crypto opportunities.

But beyond the money, Daniel had tapped into something far more valuable: empowerment. He no longer relied solely on banks or employers. He was building a personal financial system that ran 24/7, across borders, without permission. It gave him peace of mind, a sense of control, and a growing confidence in his ability to adapt to the future of money.

Crypto passive income wasn't just a strategy—it was a mindset shift.

Now, Daniel spends his free time helping others navigate the same journey. He hosts webinars for beginners, teaches family members how to use wallets safely, and even started writing a blog sharing his experiences. He knows the crypto world can be overwhelming, especially for newcomers. But he also knows that the sooner you learn how to make your money work for you, the sooner you gain time, freedom, and resilience.

His story is a reminder that financial freedom is no longer reserved for the wealthy, the connected, or the lucky. In the decentralized world, anyone with the willingness to learn, experiment, and stay cautious can build a stream of income that flows long after the initial effort. Like Daniel, you too can unlock that freedom—one step, one strategy, and one yield at a time.

Chapter 2: Staking: How to Earn Reliable Yields by Securing the Blockchain

Staking has quickly become one of the most popular and accessible ways for investors to earn passive income in crypto. The idea is elegant and powerful: you lock up your crypto to support a blockchain network—and in return, you're rewarded with additional tokens. Unlike proof-of-work systems like Bitcoin, which require energy-intensive mining, proof-of-stake (PoS) networks achieve consensus by relying on staked assets. These staked tokens help validate transactions, secure the network, and maintain decentralization. If you're just starting your crypto income journey, staking is often the safest and most straightforward entry point.

To stake, you must hold a PoS-compatible cryptocurrency. Popular staking coins include Ethereum (ETH), Cardano (ADA), Solana (SOL), Polkadot (DOT), Avalanche (AVAX), and Cosmos (ATOM). Each of these networks has its own set of rules, lock-up periods, minimum staking amounts, and reward structures. For example, Cardano allows delegation with no lock-up period, while Ethereum staking through native validators requires 32 ETH and a long withdrawal delay. However, many exchanges and DeFi platforms offer flexible staking solutions that lower the entry barrier significantly.

There are two primary staking options: **custodial staking** and **non-custodial staking**. Custodial staking is when a centralized platform—like Coinbase, Binance, or Kraken—stakes your tokens on your behalf. It's easy to use, requires no technical knowledge, and typically offers lower but reliable rewards. The downside is that you give up custody of your funds, meaning the platform holds your private keys. If it's hacked or collapses, like FTX did, your funds could be at risk. That's why many experienced crypto users prefer non-custodial staking, which involves using wallets like Ledger, Trust Wallet, or Keplr to maintain control over your private keys while still earning staking rewards.

Non-custodial staking usually works through **validator delegation**. You don't need to run a validator node yourself—instead, you delegate your tokens to a validator who does the work of processing transactions and earning block rewards. These validators take a small commission (usually between 2–10%) and pass the rest of the earnings to you. Selecting a reliable validator is crucial. Look for validators with high uptime, consistent rewards, low commission fees, and good reputations. Avoid validators with centralization concerns or history of downtime or slashing penalties.

Speaking of slashing—this is a concept unique to PoS networks where misbehaving validators (those who go offline, double-sign blocks, or cheat) are penalized by having a portion of their staked tokens "slashed," or destroyed. If you're staking through delegation, you share in that risk. Although it's rare, choosing a poor validator could lead to a reduction in your staked amount. This is why validator research is just as important as understanding the staking mechanics themselves. Sites like StakingRewards.com or ValidatorRatings.com help compare validators by performance and transparency.

Your staking rewards vary depending on the network, inflation rate, and total staked supply. Generally, you can expect between 4% to 12% APY on most major networks. For example, staking Solana might yield 6–7%, while staking Cosmos can reach 10% annually. Ethereum's current post-merge staking yield fluctuates based on network activity and is currently around 4–6%. These yields are paid in the native token of the blockchain, meaning your earnings grow in the same asset you staked. This compounds over time, especially if you re-stake your rewards periodically.

Some platforms offer **liquid staking**, a newer option that solves one of staking's biggest drawbacks—illiquidity. With traditional staking, your tokens are locked and cannot be sold or transferred until the unbonding period ends, which can range from 3 to 21 days depending on the chain. Liquid staking protocols like Lido, Rocket Pool, and Stader offer a tokenized version of your staked assets (e.g., stETH for staked ETH) that you can use across DeFi platforms. This allows you to earn staking rewards while maintaining liquidity for borrowing, trading, or providing liquidity in other protocols. However, liquid staking comes with smart contract risk, so choose platforms that have been audited and widely adopted.

From a security perspective, staking is generally safer than farming or lending. You're not actively exposing your funds to market volatility or depending on borrower behavior. However, you are still exposed to **token price fluctuation**, which can impact your total yield in fiat terms. For example, if you earn 10% APY on a coin that drops 50% in value, your real return is negative. For this reason, it's often wise to stake coins that you believe in long-term—not just for their yield, but for their fundamental value and growth potential.

Managing your staking portfolio can be done using tools and dashboards that aggregate data across networks and wallets. Apps like Zerion, DeBank, or Ledger Live make it easy to track your staking rewards, validator status, and total return over time. Some wallets even allow automatic reward compounding, so your earnings are constantly reinvested for exponential growth. Just be mindful of transaction fees, especially on networks like Ethereum where gas can eat into your profits.

Finally, as a beginner, it's best to start small. Try staking a small amount of a mid-tier coin like ADA, DOT, or ATOM through a mobile wallet with built-in staking features. As you gain confidence and see the rewards flow in, you can begin diversifying across networks and experimenting with more advanced staking strategies like validator rotation or liquid staking. Over time, staking can become a reliable and low-maintenance way to earn income while supporting the networks you believe in.

Staking is the gateway to understanding how decentralized networks function and reward participation. It's also one of the safest and most transparent methods for earning yield in the crypto economy. By learning how to stake, choosing the right assets, and managing your risks, you can build a steady income stream that grows with the future of Web3.

How Lisa discovered a better alternative investment

Lisa was a single mother in her late thirties, juggling a part-time job and raising two kids while trying to make the most of her limited income. She had always been curious about investing but found Wall Street too complex and inaccessible.

One evening, while scrolling through her phone after the kids went to bed, she came across a short video about earning interest from crypto through something called “staking.” The term was unfamiliar, but the promise of putting money to work without day trading or coding sounded exactly like what she needed.

The next day, she dove in. Lisa watched YouTube tutorials, read Reddit threads, and scanned articles explaining staking in beginner-friendly terms. She learned that staking was how certain blockchains maintained their networks—not through mining, but through users like her who locked up their tokens in exchange for rewards. The more she read, the more it made sense. She was already earning 0.01% in her bank savings account. But here was a system offering 5% or even 10% per year, just for participating in a network and holding her assets.

Lisa decided to test it out. She chose Cardano (ADA) because it didn’t require a massive upfront investment, and it offered flexible staking through delegation. She created a wallet using Yoroi, a beginner-friendly staking wallet, and transferred about $300 worth of ADA into it. At first, she was nervous—what if she sent it to the wrong address? What if the wallet got hacked? But step by step, she followed the instructions and soon found herself choosing a staking pool.

After comparing validator stats, she delegated her ADA to a pool with a high success rate and low commission.

A few days passed. Then a week. Then, one morning, she checked her wallet and saw it—her first staking reward. A small deposit of additional ADA had appeared. It wasn't a fortune, but it was more than any bank had ever given her for just saving money. And it felt different. It felt like she was finally participating in a system that wasn't rigged in someone else's favor. She wasn't paying fees to some distant institution—she was earning for helping power the very blockchain she believed in.

Encouraged, Lisa started expanding her efforts. She looked into staking Solana and Polkadot, reading about their ecosystems and deciding which ones aligned with her values and goals. She set reminders to check on her validators, rotate them when necessary, and re-delegate her rewards to maximize compounding. Over time, she built a mini staking portfolio—nothing massive, but enough to see her crypto income grow steadily every month. The best part? She could do it all from her phone during school pickup or lunch breaks.

But Lisa wasn't naïve. She learned the importance of choosing trustworthy validators after reading stories of slashing incidents. She double-checked the platforms she used, avoided flashy promises of high returns, and kept her keys secure. She even explored the idea of liquid staking, trying out stETH on Lido so she could earn rewards and still use her staked Ethereum elsewhere. The deeper she went, the more empowered she felt. This wasn't just passive income—it was financial education in action.

Eventually, Lisa began teaching others in her community. She organized small meetups at the local library to help other single parents and working-class neighbors understand staking. Some had never invested a dollar in their lives. Others were frustrated with inflation and banks. But when Lisa showed them her growing ADA rewards, the lightbulbs went off. She wasn't rich, but she had something priceless: a plan. A system. A future where her money wasn't idle—it was growing, working, and multiplying with each passing day.

Today, Lisa earns around $50 a month from staking—enough to pay her phone bill or take her kids out to a nice dinner. And that number keeps growing. What started as a late-night curiosity has become a consistent source of income and pride. More importantly, it has changed how she views money and technology. Lisa no longer feels like an outsider to investing. In fact, she's ahead of the curve—staking, compounding, and securing the next generation of financial systems, all from her living room.

Chapter 3: Yield Farming and Liquidity Pools: Earning Big With DeFi

Yield farming is often referred to as the "high-yield savings account" of DeFi, but this analogy only scratches the surface. In reality, yield farming is one of the most powerful—and complex—ways to earn passive income in crypto. By providing liquidity to decentralized exchanges (DEXs), you allow others to trade assets without a central party. In return, you earn a share of transaction fees, incentive tokens, and even bonuses from new DeFi protocols trying to bootstrap user participation. This chapter explains how yield farming works, how to set it up, and how to do it safely so you can maximize rewards without exposing yourself to unnecessary risk.

At the heart of yield farming are **liquidity pools**—smart contracts that hold two or more tokens in equal value (e.g., ETH/USDC or BNB/BUSD). When you contribute to a pool, you become a **liquidity provider (LP)**. You deposit both assets in equal value, and in return, you receive **LP tokens** that represent your share of the pool. These tokens can then be staked or used in other DeFi protocols to earn additional rewards. Yield farmers typically earn two kinds of income: (1) **trading fees** generated by user swaps on the exchange (usually 0.2%–0.3% per trade), and (2) **incentives** from DeFi platforms in the form of governance or utility tokens.

Let's break this down with a simple example. Suppose you provide $500 worth of ETH and $500 worth of USDC to the ETH/USDC pool on Uniswap. You now own a share of that pool and begin earning a percentage of the transaction fees every time someone swaps ETH for USDC or vice versa. On top of that, if Uniswap is running an incentive campaign, you might also receive UNI tokens as an additional reward. This layered income—base yield plus incentive tokens—is what makes yield farming so attractive.

However, yield farming comes with risks, the most notorious being **impermanent loss**. This happens when the price of the two tokens in your pair changes significantly after you deposit them into the pool. If, for instance, ETH doubles in price while USDC remains stable, your pool will automatically rebalance to keep both assets in equal value, meaning you'll end up with less ETH than you started with. When you withdraw your funds, the value may be lower than if you had simply held both assets separately. Impermanent loss isn't always realized, especially if trading fees and rewards make up for it—but it's critical to understand this risk before jumping into a farm.

To reduce the chance of impermanent loss, many farmers use **stablecoin pairs** (e.g., USDC/DAI or USDT/BUSD), since both tokens maintain a 1:1 value. This way, you avoid most price volatility and earn reliable fees with limited risk. Another strategy is to pair volatile tokens only when you expect them to move in the same direction or remain relatively stable against each other. Tools like ImpermanentLoss.app can help you calculate potential losses before providing liquidity.

Platforms that offer yield farming include **Uniswap, PancakeSwap, SushiSwap, Curve Finance, Balancer, and QuickSwap**—each with different ecosystems, networks, and user incentives. Some are Ethereum-based (with higher gas fees), while others operate on cheaper chains like Binance Smart Chain, Polygon, or Arbitrum. For beginners, it's often wise to start on lower-fee networks to experiment with small amounts and avoid spending $50 or more just to deposit or withdraw from a pool.

Many of these platforms also offer **farming dashboards** or **"farm-as-a-service" vaults** that automate and optimize the process for you. Tools like **Beefy Finance, Autofarm, and Yearn.Finance** automatically claim rewards, re-stake them, and shift your assets into higher-yielding pools. These vaults can significantly boost your APY, especially when auto-compounding is enabled. However, they add another layer of smart contract risk and fees, so always research vault providers and stick to platforms with strong reputations, audits, and high Total Value Locked (TVL).

A key factor in successful yield farming is **calculating true yield**. While a farm may advertise a 100% APY, you must consider whether rewards are paid in volatile tokens that can rapidly lose value. For instance, many DeFi tokens experience inflation, where more tokens are printed over time, diluting value. Always convert expected rewards into a stablecoin or fiat equivalent when evaluating opportunities. Additionally, consider farming **blue-chip pairs** like ETH/USDC or BTC/ETH rather than chasing high-APY meme coin pools that are more likely to collapse.

Another essential skill in yield farming is managing your **LP tokens**. These are the assets that represent your claim to the pool and can be used across multiple DeFi platforms for "stacked yield." For example, you might provide liquidity on Curve, receive LP tokens, and then stake them on Convex Finance for additional rewards. This multi-platform stacking allows advanced farmers to earn layered income, but it requires caution. Each additional layer increases the number of smart contracts and risks involved. Only deploy these strategies once you're confident in how the platforms operate and how to recover your assets if something goes wrong.

To keep your yield farming operations safe, follow these best practices:

- Always start with small amounts until you're familiar with the tools.
- Use audited platforms with strong developer communities and high liquidity.
- Read documentation thoroughly to understand withdrawal rules, harvest timings, and fees.
- Keep track of farming positions in spreadsheets or dashboards.
- Regularly monitor your LP token values and reward balances.

Finally, never forget the golden rule of DeFi: **never invest more than you can afford to lose**. Yield farming is a high-yield opportunity, but it is not risk-free. Protocols can be hacked, developers can abandon projects, and markets can crash overnight. Protect yourself by diversifying your strategies, using trusted tools, and continuously learning about how the ecosystem evolves.

In the next chapter, we'll explore **crypto lending**, a more conservative way to earn interest on your assets without the volatility of liquidity pools. While it may offer lower returns, it's ideal for stability and consistent growth—especially when using stablecoins or well-collateralized platforms.

Marco's Adventure Into Yield Farming

Marco was a former software engineer turned digital nomad. After years of working in high-stress tech jobs, he quit the corporate grind and began traveling across Southeast Asia. With his savings in crypto and a modest stream of freelance work, Marco sought smarter ways to grow his wealth passively. One morning, while sipping iced coffee in Chiang Mai, he overheard a conversation between two blockchain enthusiasts discussing "yield farming" and "liquidity pools." Their words were filled with excitement—and numbers that made his ears perk up. Twenty percent annual returns? Compounding strategies? It sounded too good to be true. But curiosity got the best of him.

Back at his hostel, Marco opened his laptop and dove deep. He learned that yield farming involved providing liquidity to decentralized exchanges, essentially lending his crypto into trading pools in exchange for a cut of the transaction fees and bonus rewards. The process seemed technical but logical. After reading for hours, he decided to experiment with $1,000. He split it evenly between ETH and USDC, then provided it to the

ETH/USDC pool on Uniswap. After the transaction confirmed, he received LP tokens in return—his share of the pool.

The next day, he checked his dashboard. A small amount of income had already appeared. It was thrilling. His assets were working for him—even while he slept. Energized, he began to explore more options. He moved to PancakeSwap on Binance Smart Chain to escape Ethereum's high gas fees. There, he tried stablecoin pairs like USDT/BUSD to reduce volatility. He began earning slightly less yield, but with far less stress. The smoothness and automation of DeFi began to amaze him.

But it wasn't all smooth sailing. A few weeks later, Marco made a mistake. Attracted by a new DeFi platform offering 300% APY, he added $500 into a flashy token pool. The interface was slick, and the reward token skyrocketed for a week. But then it crashed—fast. The platform was exposed as a rug pull. The developers drained the liquidity, the reward token plummeted, and Marco's funds evaporated. The sting of loss hit hard. He realized that yield farming wasn't just about chasing numbers—it was about understanding the platform, the community, and the risks.

Determined to learn from the experience, Marco refined his strategy. He began using sites like DeFi Llama and CoinGecko to research protocol credibility, TVL (total value locked), and audit history. He diversified his funds across multiple farms and stuck to blue-chip protocols like Curve, SushiSwap, and Aave. He used stablecoin-only pools when traveling for long periods and tested new yield optimizers like Yearn.Finance and Beefy with minimal funds first. He even wrote a checklist for himself before depositing funds: Is the code audited? Is the liquidity real? Who controls the smart contract?

As the months passed, Marco became proficient. He tracked his LP token values, learned to calculate impermanent loss, and understood how to harvest and restake his earnings efficiently. His crypto dashboard began to look like a farm manager's control panel—ETH/USDC here, DAI/USDT there, with automated compounding set up across three chains. He was no longer just a user. He was an operator in a decentralized financial system that paid him to be smart, cautious, and consistent.

By the end of the year, Marco's $1,000 experiment had turned into a $4,500 passive income portfolio generating around $300 per month. That income covered his housing in Bali, his meals in Vietnam, or his next ticket to Tokyo. He wasn't trading. He wasn't working full-time. He was farming yields from a laptop, with Wi-Fi and a wallet. It felt surreal—like he had found the cheat code to a digital economy that rewarded understanding and discipline over speculation and hype.

Marco now runs a blog for fellow nomads explaining yield farming strategies in plain language. He teaches them about APYs, LP tokens, vaults, and the risks that come with chasing high returns. His goal isn't to sell dreams—but to show that financial freedom through DeFi is real, if approached with caution, research, and smart diversification. In a world where central banks devalue currency and banks pay near-zero interest, Marco's crypto farm has become a passport to the life he always wanted.

Chapter 4: Lending Crypto for Interest: Safer Yields with Stable Returns

While staking and yield farming are great ways to earn crypto income, many investors seek a more conservative and stable option—one with predictable yields, limited volatility, and minimal need for active management. Enter crypto lending. By lending out your assets—especially stablecoins—you can earn consistent interest with lower risk compared to farming volatile token pairs. Crypto lending combines the foundational principle of traditional finance—earning interest on capital—with the decentralization, speed, and global access of blockchain technology. In this chapter, you'll learn how crypto lending works, where to do it, how to minimize risk, and how to optimize for yield without exposing yourself to unnecessary losses.

Crypto lending revolves around the concept of **collateralized loans**. In DeFi, borrowers must overcollateralize their positions, meaning they must deposit more value than they borrow. For example, someone might deposit $1,500 in ETH as collateral to borrow $1,000 in USDC. If the ETH price drops too much, the loan is liquidated, and the protocol repays the lenders using the collateral. As a lender, your role is to supply liquidity—your crypto—to lending pools. In return, you earn interest paid by the borrowers. The process is governed by smart contracts and doesn't require intermediaries like banks, making it faster, cheaper, and available to anyone with a wallet.

The most trusted DeFi lending platforms include **Aave, Compound, Venus, and Geist**, with billions of dollars locked in lending markets. These platforms support a range of assets, from Ethereum and stablecoins like USDC/DAI, to altcoins like LINK, MATIC, or AVAX. Lending stablecoins is often the preferred method for passive income seekers because it minimizes the risk of price swings. If you lend out USDC, for instance, you're earning 3–8% APY depending on demand, without worrying about the token's value crashing. This makes it ideal for conservative investors who want consistent income with less exposure to crypto market volatility.

To start lending, you'll need a crypto wallet (such as MetaMask or Trust Wallet), some crypto to lend (preferably stablecoins for safety), and access to a supported DeFi platform. Once connected, you simply deposit your tokens into the protocol's lending pool. These deposits are converted into interest-bearing tokens (e.g., aUSDC in Aave), which appreciate in value as interest accrues. You can withdraw your funds at any time—unless the market experiences a liquidity crunch, which is rare but possible in extreme scenarios.

Lending yields are determined by supply and demand. If many people want to borrow USDC and few supply it, interest rates rise. Conversely, if a pool is over-supplied, rates drop. This dynamic model keeps the system balanced and encourages efficient capital usage. Platforms like Aave update their interest rates in real time, and you can check these figures on their websites or dashboards like DeFi Pulse, DefiLlama, or Zapper. Some protocols also offer **incentives in the form of governance tokens** (e.g., COMP on Compound), which can boost your total return even further.

Although crypto lending is safer than many other DeFi activities, it is not without risk. The biggest concern is **protocol risk**—the chance that a smart contract bug or exploit allows malicious actors to drain the pool. While top-tier platforms undergo audits and insurance mechanisms exist, the risk is never zero. Always do your due diligence, stick with audited and time-tested protocols, and consider diversifying across platforms to spread exposure. Another risk is **liquidity risk**—if a protocol doesn't have enough liquidity available when you want to withdraw, your funds could be temporarily inaccessible. This is rare on large platforms but can happen during market panics or black swan events.

One of the smartest strategies in crypto lending is **looping with collateral**. For example, you could deposit USDC into

Aave, borrow DAI, convert DAI back into USDC, and deposit it again—looping this process to amplify your deposit base and earn higher interest. However, this technique increases risk and can lead to liquidation if collateral prices drop. It's not recommended for beginners but can be useful for experienced users looking to boost yield while maintaining careful margin control.

A more beginner-friendly strategy is **stablecoin-only lending diversification**. Allocate your capital across three or four trusted platforms using stablecoins only, track the yields monthly, and reinvest the interest. This creates a predictable and scalable income stream. Even during bear markets, this strategy holds up well, as stablecoin demand often rises during downturns when traders seek safe harbor. You can also automate this process using DeFi aggregators like Yearn.Finance, which optimizes where to lend based on the highest yield and rebalances automatically.

Many users also utilize **CeFi lending platforms** like Nexo, YouHodler, or formerly BlockFi (before its collapse). These platforms often offer higher yields and insurance, but the downside is that they hold custody of your funds. If the platform becomes insolvent or is poorly managed, your funds are at risk—just like with a failed bank. For this reason, DeFi lending is preferred by those who want full control over their assets, despite the slightly steeper learning curve.

As with any investment, tracking your performance is essential. Use dashboards like DeBank or APY.Vision to monitor interest accrual, protocol performance, and risk alerts. Many of these tools even allow you to simulate your lending strategy or compare yields across platforms. Regular reviews help you avoid stagnant capital, adjust allocations, and stay on top of new opportunities.

In the next chapter, we'll explore how these income streams—staking, yield farming, and lending—can be **automated and layered using vaults, aggregators, and smart strategies** to maximize passive income with minimal effort. By combining safe assets, optimized tools, and clear protocols, you can create a sustainable crypto income plan that scales over time.

Emma's Path to Stability with Crypto Lending

Emma had always been a cautious investor. Her portfolio leaned heavily on bonds, dividend stocks, and a decent chunk of cash savings—safe, predictable, and, admittedly, a bit boring. But with inflation rising and her savings eroding faster than expected, she started exploring alternatives. That's when she stumbled across a podcast episode titled *"Earn Interest in Crypto Without Trading."* Skeptical yet intrigued, Emma listened closely as the host introduced the idea of crypto lending. No wild trading. No meme coins. Just lending your digital dollars and earning real interest. For Emma, this sounded like the bridge between safety and innovation she'd been looking for.

The next week, she began her research. Unlike staking or yield farming—which involved volatile coins and a steep learning curve—crypto lending seemed refreshingly straightforward. She read about platforms like Aave and Compound, and how they allowed anyone to supply assets to a pool and earn interest automatically. Most compelling of all was the idea of lending **stablecoins**, digital assets pegged to the U.S. dollar. Emma had never been comfortable with crypto volatility, but stablecoins offered her a familiar reference point. She could earn 5–8% annually on assets like USDC or DAI—far beyond anything her bank savings account offered.

Emma decided to test the waters with $2,000 worth of USDC. She transferred it to her MetaMask wallet and connected to Aave. Following a few simple prompts, she deposited her USDC into the lending pool. Almost instantly, she received aUSDC tokens in her wallet—interest-bearing assets that gradually increased in value. It felt surreal. No credit checks. No bank paperwork. Just direct, algorithmic lending through smart contracts that couldn't discriminate, delay, or deny her participation.

As days turned into weeks, Emma became more confident. Her balance grew steadily. She explored other platforms like Compound and Curve, diversifying her lending across protocols. She used DeFi dashboards to track her yields and occasionally compared rates between platforms. Soon, she added DAI and Tether to her lending strategy and saw her passive income increase. Her setup was clean, low-maintenance, and gave her a comforting sense of control.

But Emma wasn't naive. She read about platform risks—smart contract bugs, liquidation spirals, and black swan events. To protect herself, she stuck to major, audited protocols and avoided lesser-known lending dApps. She also learned about CeFi lenders like BlockFi and Celsius, but after witnessing their eventual collapse, she felt justified in choosing DeFi instead. Her assets remained in her wallet. Her rules, her control.

One evening, Emma explored a more advanced strategy: looping. She read how users could deposit USDC, borrow DAI against it, swap DAI back to USDC, and repeat the process to multiply their exposure. While the math made sense, she paused. The risk of liquidation in volatile markets made her uneasy. She decided against it—for now. Her goal wasn't maximizing every penny, but maintaining a reliable passive income stream she could count on.

Over the next year, Emma's strategy matured. She set up monthly tracking spreadsheets, calculated her real returns in fiat, and even created a small emergency fund in USDC. By year-end, her stablecoin lending portfolio was generating over $100 a month—enough to pay her utilities or reinvest. She hadn't traded once. She hadn't stared at charts. And she hadn't taken on unnecessary risk. Her money had worked quietly and efficiently—just like she preferred.

Emma shared her journey with her sister, who was struggling to find ways to grow her modest savings. She helped her set up a wallet, taught her how to use Aave, and explained the importance of self-custody and gas fees. What started as a personal experiment became a family-wide transformation. Her teenage nephew even started learning about DeFi, intrigued by the idea that a 16-year-old could earn more lending stablecoins than most savings accounts paid adults.

Today, Emma continues to lend across multiple platforms, automating her deposits and withdrawing interest quarterly. Her confidence has grown, not because she's chasing flashy yields, but because she understands the rules of the game.

Crypto lending has become her anchor—a place where finance meets peace of mind. In a world filled with financial noise and economic instability, Emma has found quiet power in the blockchain's most underappreciated corner: slow, steady, and stable income through decentralized lending.

Chapter 5: Automating and Compounding Crypto Income: Smart Tools and Strategies

The true magic of passive income lies in its ability to grow over time—without demanding constant attention. In crypto, this principle becomes even more powerful through automation and compounding. While manual staking, lending, or farming is effective, layering in automation tools, yield aggregators, and strategic compounding can dramatically boost your long-term returns. This chapter explores how to streamline your crypto income through automated systems, saving time, reducing risk, and accelerating wealth growth without daily oversight.

The first core concept is **auto-compounding**, which means reinvesting your crypto rewards into the same protocol to earn interest on interest. In traditional finance, this might look like reinvesting dividends. In crypto, it often means automatically claiming rewards, swapping them for the original asset, and redepositing them into the staking pool, lending protocol, or liquidity farm. Without compounding, your earnings plateau. With it, they grow exponentially. Doing this manually is time-consuming and inefficient—especially on chains with high gas fees. That's where automation tools come in.

Yield aggregators like **Yearn.Finance**, **Beefy Finance**, **Autofarm**, **Reaper**, and **Harvest** have revolutionized passive income by handling this process automatically. These platforms identify the best DeFi protocols, deploy user funds into optimized strategies, and continually rebalance or compound rewards. For example, Beefy Finance might take your USDC/DAI LP tokens, claim trading fees and bonus tokens, swap them back into USDC/DAI, and restake them—sometimes multiple times a day. This drastically boosts your APY compared to a set-and-forget position. These services typically charge a small performance or management fee, but in most cases, the increased yield more than compensates.

Another major advantage of yield aggregators is **strategy diversification**. Many of these platforms allow users to allocate funds across multiple vaults—each with different risk levels, token pairs, and networks. You can choose low-risk stablecoin vaults, moderate-risk blue-chip farms, or high-yield experimental pools depending on your tolerance and goals. Some even use risk models to score each vault based on factors like token volatility, smart contract complexity, and past exploits.

To make automation work, you must also consider **network efficiency**. Ethereum-based platforms can cost $20–$100 per transaction, making daily auto-compounding uneconomical unless you're deploying large amounts. Layer 2s and alternative chains like **Polygon, Arbitrum, Avalanche, Fantom, and BNB Chain** offer fast, cheap transactions, which allow aggregators to perform micro-compounding regularly without draining profits. Choosing the right network is as important as choosing the right strategy. When testing an aggregator, always try with a small amount first, review vault history, and check community feedback on Twitter, Discord, or DeFiLlama.

Beyond aggregators, another automation layer involves **rebalancing tools and bots**. Protocols like **Balancer** offer dynamic portfolios that automatically adjust token allocations based on your target mix. For example, you might want a portfolio that's always 50% ETH and 50% USDC. If ETH pumps, Balancer will sell ETH to buy more USDC, maintaining your ratio and locking in gains. This strategy not only automates profit-taking but also smooths your yield across different market cycles.

Some investors use **DeFi automation platforms** like **Gelato Network, Instadapp, and DeFi Saver** to set up more complex instructions. These can include conditional actions like "if token price drops 20%, move funds to stablecoin vault" or "if gas fees fall below a threshold, harvest and restake." With these tools, your crypto income strategy begins to resemble a robo-advisor—one tailored by you and executed by code 24/7. While advanced, these tools require caution. Always double-check logic, test with small amounts, and make sure the protocol is audited and battle-tested.

Don't forget the **manual automation layer** you can apply by setting up reminders, using spreadsheets, or syncing with tracking dashboards like **Zapper, DeBank, Zerion, or APY.Vision**. These tools help you track vault performance, estimate real-time yield, and get notified about changes in APY or protocol status. A weekly or monthly review can go a long way in making small tweaks that improve long-term results.

For those who want maximum hands-off income, a **DeFi basket strategy** can be ideal. This involves allocating 25–50% to auto-compounding vaults, 25% to stablecoin lending protocols, and the rest to safe staking positions. Over time, this blend generates diversified, steady, and compounding returns, all while minimizing single-point-of-failure risk. With quarterly reviews and occasional reallocations, this system can function nearly autonomously—earning yield on autopilot.

Security remains key when automating. Always use **hardware wallets** like Ledger or Trezor to approve transactions and store vault LP tokens or interest-bearing tokens. Never give smart contracts unlimited token approvals. Set spending limits and revoke permissions using tools like Revoke.cash. If you use Telegram or Discord for DeFi groups, avoid clicking unknown links and double-check every URL. Automation doesn't eliminate risk—it amplifies both your gains and your exposure.

In the final part of this chapter, remember that **simplicity scales**. Many investors overcomplicate strategies chasing every new farm or APY. Instead, the highest long-term earners are those who build a consistent system, automate smartly, and stay informed without becoming obsessed. Your time is valuable. Use automation to free it. Let crypto work for you—not the other way around.

In the next chapter, we'll explore **layering multiple income streams together**—combining staking, lending, and yield farming in a smart, diversified portfolio that minimizes volatility while maximizing cash flow.

Jason Builds a Crypto Machine That Runs Itself

Jason was an operations manager by day and a productivity nerd by night. His bookshelf overflowed with titles on automation, system design, and financial independence. When he discovered crypto, he saw it not just as a way to invest—but as a system he could optimize. While others chased moonshot tokens or followed influencer trades, Jason was intrigued by something else: earning passive income through staking, lending, and yield farming—and automating the entire process like clockwork.

It started with a simple idea: "If my money can earn money, and then that money can earn more money without me lifting a finger—that's real freedom." Jason began building what he called his *Crypto Income Engine*. He didn't want to spend his evenings harvesting farm rewards or checking interest rates. He wanted to set it, forget it, and let it grow.

He began with **Beefy Finance**, testing a stablecoin vault that auto-compounded his USDC/DAI LP tokens. He deposited $2,000 and watched as the dashboard showed his earnings grow in real time. Every few hours, the vault harvested, swapped, and restaked his rewards automatically. It was the first time Jason felt like crypto was doing the work for him. Encouraged, he diversified into **Yearn.Finance**, allocating funds to vaults that optimized lending strategies across Aave, Compound, and Curve. Each vault operated like a smart assistant, constantly rebalancing for the highest yield.

But Jason wasn't content with just plugging into vaults. He wanted transparency. He began using tools like **Zapper** and

DeBank to monitor his portfolio's performance. He built a spreadsheet that pulled in APY changes weekly. He added rules: if a vault dropped below a certain yield, he'd reallocate. If gas fees exceeded a set threshold, he'd wait to harvest. Over time, his income engine became an elegant web of logic and automation—earning interest on interest, diversified across risk levels and chains.

As Jason's knowledge grew, so did his ambition. He explored platforms like **Balancer**, where he created a dynamic portfolio that maintained a 60/40 ETH-to-stablecoin ratio. If ETH surged, the pool rebalanced, locking in profits automatically. He then discovered **Gelato Network**, which let him create rules like "harvest if gas is below 50 gwei" or "move rewards to a cold wallet once they exceed $100." These smart contracts became his digital workers—on call 24/7.

To secure everything, Jason stored his assets in a **Ledger hardware wallet**, only approving spending caps for specific contracts. He regularly used **Revoke.cash** to clear old approvals and kept a printed list of critical wallet recovery phrases in a locked safe. He even wrote out a short document for his wife in case anything happened to him, explaining how to access and unwind the system safely.

What truly set Jason apart was his mindset. He didn't chase the hottest new farm. He didn't gamble on unknown tokens. He focused on consistency. By reinvesting earnings, keeping fees low, and using platforms with high total value locked and audits, he earned an average of 18% APY across his crypto income machine—with minimal effort. Every month, he funneled his profits into either a Bitcoin cold wallet for long-term savings or a prepaid card that let him spend stablecoins like cash.

Eventually, Jason built a dashboard for others to copy. He gave talks at local meetups, sharing his automation strategies with other nine-to-fivers who wanted crypto income without becoming full-time DeFi traders. Some of them followed his setup step by step and began seeing results within weeks. His system didn't make anyone rich overnight—but it gave them predictability, control, and peace of mind in an otherwise chaotic crypto world.

Today, Jason checks his dashboard once a week, just like he'd check a thermostat. His system runs quietly, adjusting and compounding in the background. What started as a side experiment has become a full-on digital income engine—one that frees up his time to travel, play music, and spend weekends with his family. He no longer works for money every day. Now, his money works for him—and does it better than any job he's ever had.

Chapter 6: Building a Diversified Crypto Income Portfolio: Balance, Safety, and Scale

Once you've explored staking, lending, and yield farming individually, the next logical step is to build a **diversified passive income portfolio**—a structured system that combines all these strategies in balance. Diversification is a foundational principle in traditional investing, and it's even more critical in the volatile world of cryptocurrency. By spreading your funds across different income sources, networks, assets, and risk levels, you reduce your exposure to any single point of failure and create a more stable and scalable income stream. This chapter will walk you through designing your own crypto income blueprint.

The first principle is **asset-type diversification**. Not all crypto assets are created equal. Some are volatile (like ETH or AVAX), others are stablecoins (like USDC or DAI), and others are governance tokens or staking coins. A smart portfolio might allocate 40–50% to stablecoins for predictable yield, 25–35% to blue-chip tokens like ETH or BTC for long-term growth and staking, and the remainder to higher-yield but riskier assets like LP tokens or DeFi protocol tokens. This ensures that even during down markets, your stablecoins continue to earn, while your riskier assets have upside potential during bull runs.

Next, you'll want to diversify by **strategy**. Allocate some funds to **staking** for low-maintenance, long-term growth. These positions can be set once and left untouched for months. Ethereum, Cardano, and Polkadot are excellent staking assets. Then use stablecoins for **lending**, which provides consistent returns regardless of market direction. Lending platforms like Aave, Compound, and Curve offer reliable yield on USDC, USDT, and DAI with relatively low risk. Lastly, allocate a portion to **yield farming**—either through automated vaults or direct LP positions—for higher returns. This portion requires closer monitoring, but the rewards can be significant when done correctly.

Another essential form of diversification is **platform-level diversification**. Don't put all your assets on a single DeFi protocol. Even the most secure platforms can be hacked or experience bugs. Split your staking between platforms like Lido and Rocket Pool. Spread your stablecoin lending across Aave, Compound, and Yearn. Distribute your LP tokens between Uniswap, PancakeSwap, and Curve. This way, even if one protocol experiences an issue, the majority of your portfolio remains unaffected. Use tools like DeFiLlama or Token Terminal to analyze platform metrics like Total Value

Locked (TVL), audit status, and usage history to make informed decisions.

It's also important to think in terms of **time diversification**. Not every strategy pays out on the same schedule. Staking rewards might be paid weekly, lending interest accrues daily, and farming yields can be harvested hourly or in real time. Design your system so that income is flowing in at various intervals. This allows you to reinvest more frequently, respond to market shifts, and smooth out your cash flow. If you're building toward regular crypto income (e.g., $500/month), having staggered returns gives you more flexibility in spending or reinvesting.

A well-balanced income portfolio also includes **risk-adjusted allocations**. High APY doesn't always mean better. In fact, many protocols offering 100%+ returns often pay in highly inflationary tokens with little value retention. Assess risk by asking:

- Is the asset volatile or stable?
- Is the protocol audited and reputable?
- What's the smart contract risk level?
- How much liquidity is in the platform?

- How many users are actively earning from it?

If a strategy scores poorly on these criteria, reduce your exposure to it. Conversely, assets and platforms with long histories, active communities, and large TVL can be given a higher weight. Use the **Core-Satellite Model**: 70–80% of your portfolio in stable, low-risk assets and platforms (your core), and 20–30% in high-yield, experimental or newer opportunities (your satellites).

You can also add **geographic and regulatory diversification** by spreading assets across blockchains. Ethereum is the most established but has high fees. Binance Smart Chain offers low costs and speed but is more centralized. Polygon, Avalanche, Arbitrum, and Fantom offer cost-effective DeFi ecosystems with growing reliability. Holding assets and earning yield on multiple chains not only protects you from single-chain congestion or outages, but also gives you access to more vaults, farms, and lending options.

For easier management, set up a **crypto income dashboard** using DeBank, Zapper, or Zerion. These platforms aggregate your positions across wallets and protocols, showing total value, yield, and performance. You can also use a Google Sheet or Notion tracker to manually update yields, compound frequency, and rebalance schedules. Reviewing your portfolio monthly or quarterly is key to staying aligned with your goals and avoiding overexposure to declining assets.

Finally, define your **income goal**. Are you trying to earn an extra $200/month to cover bills? Or aiming to generate a full-time crypto income of $2,000/month? Based on your goal, reverse-engineer your portfolio allocations. For example, earning $200/month at an average yield of 10% APY requires $24,000 in deployed capital. If you can only allocate $12,000, you'll need to find higher-yielding—but balanced—strategies or accept a slower path to your goal.

Your diversified portfolio isn't just about protecting wealth—it's about making passive income consistent and scalable. By balancing your assets, platforms, and risk levels, you create a self-sustaining system that thrives across market cycles. The next chapter will explore how to protect and insure your crypto income—ensuring that your digital cash flow remains resilient against hacks, volatility, and black swan events.

Nina's Balanced Crypto Income Portfolio

Nina was a 42-year-old marketing consultant who had grown weary of the financial roller coaster. After surviving two layoffs, volatile stock investments, and watching interest rates eat away at her savings, she decided it was time to take control.

Crypto had always fascinated her, but the chaos and complexity had kept her away—until she discovered the world of passive income. Her goal wasn't to become a crypto millionaire. She wanted stability, predictability, and a steady stream of income to support her freelance lifestyle. That's when she decided to build a diversified crypto income portfolio.

Nina started with research. She wasn't interested in moonshot meme coins or 1,000% APYs. She wanted to build a system—one that combined reliability and growth. She laid out her goals in a simple spreadsheet: $300/month in crypto income, ideally from different sources and assets. With $20,000 to deploy, she needed to earn an average return of 18% APY, and she wasn't going to rely on one method to get there. She began dividing her portfolio across three pillars: staking, lending, and yield farming.

She allocated 40% of her funds—$8,000—to **stablecoin lending**. Safety was her priority here. Using Aave and Compound, she deposited USDC and DAI, which generated between 5% and 8% interest. She appreciated the simplicity. No price volatility, no sleepless nights, just slow and steady income. She spread her stablecoins across two protocols and set a calendar reminder to check performance once a week.

With $8,000 earning at an average of 6%, she was generating about $40/month from this portion alone.

Next, she staked $6,000 in **blue-chip cryptocurrencies**: Ethereum on Lido, Cardano on Yoroi, and a small position in Avalanche on her Ledger wallet. The yields weren't astronomical—around 4% to 8%—but the assets were strong, and she was happy to hold them long term. She considered this her "sleep well at night" section. Her staking setup was mostly automated, and the rewards were steadily accumulating. This layer gave her exposure to potential long-term gains while also earning short-term passive yield.

For the final $6,000, Nina wanted higher returns. She dipped into **yield farming**, starting cautiously with a USDC/USDT liquidity pair on Curve Finance. Then she explored an auto-compounding vault on Beefy Finance using a BTC/ETH LP. She avoided obscure farms, choosing protocols with audits and high Total Value Locked. The returns were impressive—over 20% APY in some cases—but she knew the risks, like impermanent loss and smart contract exploits. To mitigate them, she never kept more than $2,000 in any one farm and checked her positions weekly. This part of her portfolio fluctuated more, but it also drove most of her yield.

After setting up her three-part system, Nina realized the true power of diversification. One month, when her yield farm returns dipped due to market volatility, her lending interest and staking rewards kept flowing. During a market upswing, her staked ETH appreciated significantly, while her stablecoins held steady value. No matter what happened in the market, part of her system was always working in her favor.

Nina used Zapper and DeBank to track her positions. She created a Notion dashboard to log weekly performance and wrote quarterly notes to herself about what was working and what to tweak. Over time, her portfolio stabilized into a well-oiled machine. After six months, she had earned over $1,000 in passive income—reinvested into her highest-performing strategies.

What surprised Nina most was how manageable it all became. In the beginning, it felt like learning a new language. But with time, practice, and a commitment to staying conservative, she had built something that many people never discover: a portfolio that paid her without draining her time or emotions. She no longer feared inflation, job instability, or market crashes. Her income was diversified, automated, and scalable.

By the end of her first year, Nina was earning just over $350/month. She treated it as her "freedom fund"—money that gave her room to breathe between clients, take trips, or invest in her creative passions. And best of all, it didn't come from luck or timing the market—it came from thoughtful structure, smart diversification, and steady execution.

Chapter 7: Managing Risk and Protecting Your Crypto Income

Earning passive income in crypto offers enormous upside—but with it comes a unique set of risks. Unlike traditional finance, where systems are regulated, insured, and time-tested, decentralized finance (DeFi) operates in a relatively new and fast-moving environment. Security breaches, token crashes, and smart contract exploits can erase months—or years—of gains in moments. That's why managing risk is just as important as choosing high-yield opportunities. This chapter covers the key risks in crypto income strategies and provides practical tools and techniques to help you protect your digital cash flow.

The first and most common danger is **smart contract risk**. DeFi protocols are powered by code, not people. If that code has vulnerabilities—and many do—it can be exploited by hackers. When you stake coins, provide liquidity, or lend funds, you're trusting that the smart contract will execute correctly and securely. If an exploit occurs, you could lose all your deposited assets. To mitigate this risk, only use protocols that have undergone **multiple audits by respected firms**, have open-source code, and have been live for a long time with high Total Value Locked (TVL). Avoid new projects that offer flashy returns without a proven track record or community trust.

Another major risk is **impermanent loss**—unique to liquidity providers. As covered in Chapter 3, if the prices of the tokens you've deposited diverge too much in either direction, you may suffer a loss compared to simply holding the tokens. Many investors underestimate this. Tools like impermanentloss.app can help you calculate expected loss before committing to a farm. To reduce exposure, stick with stablecoin pairs or asset pairs that tend to move together (e.g., ETH/wETH or USDC/DAI). And remember, impermanent loss is only "impermanent" if prices return to the original ratio. Otherwise, it becomes permanent when you withdraw your funds.

Volatility risk is another concern. Many yield farming and staking rewards are paid in volatile native tokens. Even if you're earning 80% APY in token rewards, it means little if the token drops 90% in value. Always assess yield in **real terms**—convert projected token rewards into stablecoin or fiat value, and ask yourself if it's worth the exposure. This is why many income-focused investors prefer stablecoin lending: it provides reliable returns without worrying about token crashes. That said, for those willing to accept more volatility, higher rewards may justify holding a portion of riskier tokens.

Platform risk refers to the overall reliability and safety of a DeFi platform. If the development team disappears, if governance is overtaken by bad actors, or if core developers introduce bugs, the entire protocol could collapse. To mitigate this, look at protocol transparency, the strength of their community, DAO governance activity, and whether the founders are known and reputable. Social proof, GitHub activity, and Twitter/Discord community size are useful indicators. Projects like Aave, Curve, and Lido have strong, battle-tested reputations—newer or obscure platforms should be approached with skepticism.

Next, you must consider **rug pull risk**. This occurs when developers or insiders withdraw all the liquidity from a pool or vault, leaving investors with worthless tokens. Rug pulls are common on unaudited, new protocols and are especially rampant on fast-moving chains like BNB Chain or Avalanche. Avoid platforms that:

- Have anonymous founders.
- Lack audits or documentation.
- Don't lock developer liquidity.
- Promote unsustainable APYs (e.g., 1,000%+). If something seems too good to be true, it usually is.

Beyond platform-specific risks, you also need to protect yourself from **operational risks**. This includes losing access to wallets, accidentally sending funds to the wrong address, or getting phished by fake websites. Use **hardware wallets** (like Ledger or Trezor) to store long-term funds and to interact with DeFi dApps more securely. Always double-check URLs, especially for popular platforms—many phishing attacks clone the interfaces of legitimate sites. Use browser extensions like **MetaMask** with built-in phishing detection, and consider creating **separate wallets** for farming, long-term holding, and experimentation.

Another overlooked risk is **gas inefficiency and fee exposure**. If you're operating on Ethereum mainnet and using small amounts of capital, your fees could consume all your profits. Consider using Layer 2 chains or alternative blockchains where gas is cheaper, such as Polygon, Arbitrum, or Fantom. Some aggregators even allow auto-compounding only when gas falls below a certain level. Timing transactions when fees are low and batching actions together helps preserve your net returns.

You should also plan for **emergencies and recovery**. Keep your seed phrases stored offline, ideally in a fireproof, waterproof safe. Never store them on cloud services or digital notepads that could be hacked. Set up a recovery plan for your family or executor in case of death or incapacitation—especially if you've built a sizable passive income system. If your wallet becomes compromised, tools like Revoke.cash and emergency withdrawal contracts (offered by some protocols) can help secure your funds quickly.

For higher-level protection, consider **DeFi insurance**. Protocols like **Nexus Mutual, InsurAce, and Unslashed Finance** offer smart contract cover, exchange hacks insurance, and yield protocol protection. Premiums are paid monthly or yearly, and claims are processed through DAO voting or claims assessors. Insurance can be expensive but may be worth it for large portfolios or high-risk farms. Just like traditional insurance, the goal isn't to get a payout—it's to sleep better knowing your downside is partially covered.

Finally, apply **position sizing rules**. Never risk more than 1–5% of your portfolio on any single protocol, no matter how promising. Set stop-loss thresholds. If a token drops more than 50% in a short time, consider exiting or reallocating. Avoid FOMO, and maintain a long-term mindset. The goal is not to make a killing overnight—but to build resilient, repeatable, scalable income.

Risk is unavoidable in crypto—but it is manageable. By staying diversified, informed, and prepared, you can reduce the probability and impact of losses. In the next chapter, we'll explore how to track your crypto income, measure your progress, and reinvest intelligently for maximum compounding and consistent growth.

How Malik Protected His Crypto Income from Disaster

Malik had always been a calculated risk-taker. As a former military engineer turned remote tech consultant, he appreciated systems that were efficient, but above all—secure. So when he entered the world of crypto passive income, he approached it the same way he had approached mission planning: with precision, backups, and a plan for every contingency. His portfolio was performing well. Between lending, staking, and yield farming, he had reached over $600 per month in passive income. But he knew that growth without protection was fragile. He needed a way to safeguard what he had built.

His first scare came when a friend's wallet was drained after connecting to a malicious farming site. The loss was instant—and total. Malik had always used MetaMask on his browser, but after that incident, he ordered a Ledger hardware wallet and began moving all his core funds offline. It changed everything. Now, every staking deposit, farm interaction, and yield withdrawal required confirmation on a physical device. It added 30 seconds to every action, but gave him peace of mind worth far more.

Next, he looked into smart contract risk. He had been farming on two platforms that promised high returns but hadn't undergone audits. A nagging feeling made him exit just in time—one of them got exploited, draining millions. From then on, Malik committed to using only audited protocols with long-standing reputations. He stuck to Curve, Aave, and Lido for most of his yield strategies, and used DeFiLlama and RugDoc to vet every new platform. If it wasn't transparent, backed by a strong community, or battle-tested, he passed.

But that wasn't enough. Malik learned about **impermanent loss** the hard way. He had provided liquidity to a high-yield AVAX/USDC pair, only to see the AVAX price crash while USDC held steady. His farming rewards barely offset the losses. Afterward, he built an impermanent loss calculator into his spreadsheet to estimate real risk before entering any LP. Eventually, he limited his LP positions to stablecoin pairs and blue-chip pairs like ETH/BTC, unless he was using vaults with loss mitigation features.

He also discovered **Revoke.cash**, a simple tool that showed all the permissions his wallet had granted. He was shocked. Dozens of old farming contracts still had permission to spend his tokens. Malik revoked them all and added a monthly reminder to check for new approvals. He adjusted his MetaMask settings to never approve unlimited token spending again—only what was needed for each transaction.

Realizing that even the best protocols can fail, Malik explored DeFi insurance. He paid a monthly premium to Nexus Mutual to insure his ETH staked with Lido and USDC lent on Aave. Some of his friends thought he was being overly cautious—but Malik saw it as paying for peace of mind. Just like homeowners insure their houses, he was insuring his passive income stream. The potential downside of not having coverage far outweighed the small monthly cost.

For extra layers of security, he kept a laminated seed phrase hidden in a safety deposit box, and a second backup at a trusted family member's home. He set up a crypto "emergency binder" with step-by-step instructions for his wife in case anything happened to him—wallet passwords, platform guides, and even notes on what to cash out first. He hoped it would never be needed, but he refused to leave his family unprepared.

Even his on-chain activity followed a security-first mindset. He created separate wallets for staking, farming, and experimentation. If one was compromised, the others remained safe. He tested new platforms with tiny amounts before deploying real capital. He used Telegram and Discord only in view-only mode and never clicked links from strangers. Every move was logged, reviewed, and justified.

Despite all his precautions, Malik wasn't paranoid. In fact, he felt freer than ever. His system didn't slow him down—it empowered him. While others chased the next 1,000% yield, Malik slept peacefully, knowing he wasn't overexposed or vulnerable. His income continued to grow steadily, and more importantly, he could count on it not being wiped out by a single mistake.

Today, Malik runs a YouTube channel teaching others how to build safe crypto income portfolios. His motto? **"Build slow, earn steady, and protect everything."** In a world where speed and greed often lead to ruin, Malik's story is a powerful reminder that resilience—not risk—is the real key to long-term passive income.

Chapter 8: Tracking, Reinvesting, and Scaling Your Crypto Income

Passive income isn't just about earning—it's about measuring, optimizing, and reinvesting to scale. As your crypto income streams grow, so does the complexity of managing them. You may have funds spread across multiple wallets, chains, platforms, and assets. Without proper tracking, it becomes difficult to assess what's working, where risks are emerging, and how to strategically reinvest for faster growth. In this chapter, we'll cover how to build a system that tracks every income stream, calculates net yield, and enables smart reinvestment decisions to grow your crypto cash flow like a real business.

Start with **centralized tracking tools** that monitor all your DeFi activity in one place. Platforms like **Zapper**, **DeBank**, **Zerion**, and **Rotki** allow you to connect your wallet(s) and view your holdings, farming positions, staked assets, and lending balances across multiple protocols and blockchains. These dashboards provide real-time portfolio snapshots, APY estimates, net worth in fiat or stablecoins, and even historical charts of income growth. Zapper, for instance, can show the exact vaults or pools you're in, while DeBank gives a breakdown of earnings over time.

Once you have visibility, the next step is **organizing your income streams**. Create a spreadsheet or Notion table that logs:

- Asset type (e.g., USDC, ETH, LP token)
- Strategy (staking, lending, yield farming)
- Platform used (Aave, Curve, Lido, Beefy, etc.)
- Chain (Ethereum, Polygon, Arbitrum, etc.)
- Initial capital invested
- Current value
- Monthly yield (in tokens and USD equivalent)
- APY or APR
- Notes on risk level, lock-up period, and next review date

Updating this tracker weekly or monthly gives you a clear view of which positions are outperforming and which may need to be exited or reallocated. It also helps you track how much actual income you're generating—not just paper gains. Without tracking, you're flying blind. With it, you're operating like a pro.

An essential part of scaling is **reinvestment**. Rather than withdrawing your crypto income to spend immediately, consider compounding it into your highest-performing strategies. For example, if your Curve stablecoin pool is earning consistent 9% APY and has low risk, reinvest interest from staking or lending into that pool. This snowballs your earnings and can double your income over time. Tools like **Beefy Finance** or **Yearn** automate compounding, but even if you're doing it manually, schedule periodic reinvestments based on gas fees and platform lock-up conditions.

You should also set **income buckets** to keep your strategy balanced:

- **Compounding bucket**: Capital and interest reinvested into existing strategies.
- **Safety bucket**: A portion of earnings (e.g., 20%) converted to stablecoins and kept in cold storage or low-risk protocols.
- **Growth bucket**: Capital reserved for exploring new farms, protocols, or staking opportunities.
- **Spending bucket**: If you're relying on crypto income for bills or lifestyle expenses, allocate a monthly withdrawal that aligns with your financial goals.

Reinvesting doesn't always mean growing exposure to the same platform. You can reinvest into **complementary strategies** to diversify. For instance, take rewards from staking and use them to buy stablecoins for lending. Or convert farm rewards into ETH and delegate them to a new validator. The more interconnected your strategy becomes, the more efficient—and resilient—it is.

Another important factor in scaling is **chain management**. As you expand across Ethereum, Arbitrum, Avalanche, and Polygon, you'll need to monitor gas fees, bridge costs, and native token balances (for gas payments). Use bridges like Hop, Synapse, or Stargate to move assets between chains. Track your assets with chain-aware dashboards like Zapper or Rabby Wallet. As your income strategy becomes multi-chain, consider syncing activities on weekends or when gas is lowest to reduce fees.

To reduce friction and increase income velocity, many users set up **automation cycles**. For example, a monthly task list might include:

- Claim and restake farming rewards.
- Rebalance LP tokens if necessary.
- Exit low-yielding or underperforming protocols.

- Review new vaults or strategies launched on trusted platforms.
- Move profits to cold storage or stablecoin savings pools.

Automation platforms like **DeFi Saver**, **Instadapp**, or **Gelato Network** can handle some of this via on-chain triggers or pre-set conditions. This allows for semi-passive scaling without needing to be online 24/7.

You also need to measure **net yield after costs**. Many investors forget to factor in:

- Gas fees (especially on Ethereum mainnet)
- Slippage during swaps
- Performance or management fees (common in vault platforms)
- Token price drops (especially with high-APY farms paid in volatile assets)

Calculating your true **Net Effective APY**—your yield minus all associated costs—helps you decide which strategies are worth continuing. For example, if you're earning 18% on a farm but paying 8% annually in gas and fees, you're really earning 10%. In contrast, a 10% APY stablecoin vault with almost no fees may offer a better long-term return.

To scale your income meaningfully, consider setting **monthly growth targets**. You might aim to increase your total crypto income by 5–10% per month through reinvestment and strategic rotation. Track this as a key metric, alongside your total capital at work and your effective yield. Small improvements, compounded consistently, lead to exponential results.

Finally, don't ignore your **exit and cash-out strategies**. Crypto income is only useful if it can eventually be used. Set up off-ramps via regulated exchanges, stablecoin debit cards, or crypto-to-fiat accounts like Coinbase or Revolut. Designate a portion of your income to convert into stablecoins or fiat monthly. If your goal is financial freedom, you need to be able to spend the money—not just watch it grow on a screen.

Tracking, reinvesting, and scaling turn a passive income experiment into a true income engine. In the next chapter, we'll explore the **future of passive income in crypto**—emerging trends like liquid staking derivatives, real-world asset tokenization, and how AI and automation will reshape income strategies in the years to come.

Olivia Tracks, Optimizes, and Scales Her Crypto Cash Flow

Olivia was a former accountant turned digital creator. Her YouTube channel on personal finance had gained traction, and as she earned more, she wanted to put her idle money to work—quietly and smartly. She had already dipped into staking and stablecoin lending, earning a few hundred dollars a month. But it wasn't until she sat down to review her year that she realized something critical: she had no clear system. Her assets were scattered across wallets, platforms, and chains, and she had no idea which income streams were performing well—or wasting her time.

Determined to bring structure to her chaos, Olivia turned her finance know-how into a personal crypto income dashboard. First, she connected her MetaMask wallet to **Zapper** and **DeBank**, instantly seeing all her assets across Ethereum, Polygon, and Arbitrum. She saw staked ETH in Lido, USDC in Aave, and LP tokens in Curve—plus a few experimental vaults she had forgotten about. The clarity was eye-opening. Her portfolio looked like a scattered closet. It was time to organize.

She created a Google Sheet that listed each position, strategy type, protocol, chain, and APY. She noted the capital invested, current value, and estimated monthly yield in USD. She color-coded her sheet: green for stable yields, yellow for volatile ones, and red for underperformers. Within an hour,

Olivia knew which strategies deserved more capital and which ones she would wind down. One farm, in particular, was producing only 3% after fees. She pulled her funds and moved them into a more efficient Beefy vault with auto-compounding.

Next, she set up a reinvestment cycle. Each month, she'd harvest all farm rewards and stablecoin lending interest, then divide it into three buckets:

1. **Compound** — reinvest into best-performing yield strategies.
2. **Secure** — convert 20% into USDC and deposit into her cold wallet.
3. **Explore** — use 10% for testing new opportunities on emerging platforms.

This rotation became a ritual. On the last Sunday of each month, she logged her income, rebalanced her assets, and moved profits as planned. Within three months, she was earning more with less capital—simply by consolidating and compounding into what actually worked.

Olivia also automated her tracking. She used **Zapper** to monitor performance daily and set up Notion reminders for her rebalancing dates. She added links to protocol dashboards, bridge tools, and even tax calculators. Everything lived in one simple but powerful dashboard she could access from her phone or laptop.

To manage risk while scaling, she created "weight caps" per protocol. No single platform would hold more than 25% of her funds. She set gas fee alerts and only harvested or moved assets when Ethereum gas dropped below 30 gwei. On chains like Polygon and Arbitrum, she felt freer to act more often, due to the low transaction cost.

But the real magic happened when Olivia began **scaling with goals**. She wanted to reach $1,000/month in passive crypto income in 12 months. So she reverse-engineered it: with an average yield of 15%, she would need roughly $80,000 working efficiently. She tracked how much new capital she was deploying each month, and how each reinvestment inched her closer to that goal. Some months she grew by $50, others by $300, depending on markets and promotions. But she could see her progress—and it kept her motivated.

Olivia also built her own "Crypto Income Reports" for her YouTube channel. Without revealing exact numbers, she shared her strategies, performance graphs, and lessons learned. The feedback was phenomenal. Thousands of viewers thanked her for showing a calm, structured approach to crypto income—something that felt attainable instead of speculative.

Over time, Olivia added new tools to her system: **APY.Vision** for yield analysis, **Revoke.cash** for contract permissions, and **LayerZero bridge** for moving assets more affordably. She even experimented with DeFi automation using **DeFi Saver**—setting a rule to auto-claim and restake farming rewards when gas prices dropped below a threshold. The machine she built didn't just run—it evolved.

One year later, Olivia hit her goal: $1,000/month in crypto passive income, diversified across staking, lending, and farming. It wasn't from chasing hype or timing the market. It came from tracking, optimizing, and scaling a system—just like a business would. And now, she wasn't just creating content about money. She was living proof that crypto income, managed smartly, could be real, reliable, and even life-changing.

Chapter 9: The Future of Crypto Passive Income: Trends, Tech, and Opportunities Ahead

The crypto income landscape is rapidly evolving. What began with simple staking and lending has transformed into a dynamic ecosystem driven by innovation in decentralized finance (DeFi), real-world asset tokenization, liquid staking derivatives, and AI-powered automation. Understanding the future of crypto passive income isn't just about keeping up—it's about staying ahead, preparing for shifts, and positioning yourself to benefit from emerging opportunities before the crowd. This chapter explores the most important trends shaping the next generation of passive crypto income.

One of the biggest shifts already underway is the **rise of liquid staking derivatives (LSDs)**. Platforms like **Lido, Rocket Pool, and Frax** now allow users to stake assets (like ETH) and receive liquid tokens (like stETH or rETH) that can be used elsewhere in DeFi. This solves a major problem: in traditional staking, your funds are locked. With LSDs, your staked asset becomes productive across multiple layers. For example, you could stake ETH with Lido to earn 4%, then use the stETH on Curve to earn trading fees, and even deposit it into lending platforms like Aave for additional APY. As LSD adoption grows, new integrations will allow these tokens to be used for farming, collateralization, and advanced yield strategies—all while still earning base staking rewards.

Another fast-growing trend is the **tokenization of real-world assets (RWAs)**. DeFi platforms are starting to offer tokenized versions of treasury bills, real estate shares, invoice-backed loans, and even gold. Protocols like **Ondo Finance**, **Maple Finance**, and **Centrifuge** are leading the charge. These RWAs generate yield from traditional off-chain sources but are wrapped into DeFi-native tokens. For investors seeking more stable and inflation-resistant income streams, this opens new doors. Imagine earning 5% from U.S. treasury-backed stablecoins, or farming yield using real estate cash flows—all on-chain. As regulation becomes clearer, RWA adoption could drive a massive new wave of passive income protocols.

Automated income protocols powered by AI are also beginning to emerge. These tools optimize yield strategies based on real-time data, sentiment, and user goals. For example, AI could analyze thousands of yield vaults across chains and automatically rotate your capital into the most profitable and secure positions. Some experimental dApps are already integrating AI prompts into DeFi frontends, helping users set strategy rules like, "Rebalance when stablecoin dominance increases," or "Exit pool if APY drops below X% for three days." As this tech matures, AI-driven passive income systems could become the DeFi equivalent of robo-advisors—automating everything from asset allocation to risk reduction.

Next comes the continued rise of **modular and cross-chain DeFi**. In the past, most strategies were siloed to a single chain like Ethereum. Now, with the growth of cross-chain bridges (like LayerZero, Axelar, and Stargate) and modular platforms like Cosmos and Polkadot, income strategies can span multiple ecosystems. You might earn staking rewards on Cosmos, lend on Ethereum Layer 2, and farm on Solana—all while managing it from a single dashboard. As interoperability improves, expect income protocols that automatically deploy capital to the chain with the best yield and lowest fees. This cross-chain yield optimization will become the norm, not the exception.

Another underappreciated trend is the integration of **passive income into wallets and exchanges**. Leading wallets like **Rabby, Zerion, and Trust Wallet** are building in yield tools that allow users to earn income with one click. Centralized exchanges are also offering DeFi-as-a-service: you deposit stablecoins, and the platform manages the yield strategy behind the scenes. While this reduces transparency, it dramatically increases accessibility for newcomers. The future will likely see embedded income features in all major wallets and fintech apps, making yield farming and staking as simple as enabling an autopilot setting.

As crypto matures, **regulation** will also reshape the income landscape. KYC requirements may become mandatory for RWA and centralized yield services. Insurance protocols may expand, offering better protection for stakers and lenders. Stablecoin regulation will likely lead to more trusted, regulated yield options backed by real-world reserves. While some current DeFi farms may disappear under legal scrutiny, new income models with clearer protections and investor safeguards will emerge. The most successful income protocols will balance decentralization with compliance, offering both security and freedom.

Looking even further ahead, we'll likely see the growth of **NFT-based income systems**, **on-chain work marketplaces**, and even **AI agents that farm yield for you autonomously**. Imagine owning an NFT that represents a share of a revenue-generating data marketplace, or running an AI bot that earns income by performing microtasks on a decentralized network. These innovations push the definition of "passive income" beyond capital alone—into the realm of network participation, computation, and ownership in entirely new digital economies.

For the average investor, what does this mean today? It means building income strategies that are:

- **Flexible**: Use liquid staking and stablecoins that can be moved across protocols.
- **Layered**: Combine multiple yield streams—staking, farming, lending—on and off chain.
- **Resilient**: Include real-world asset exposure, automated tracking, and emergency exit plans.
- **Scalable**: Structure your income like a business, with regular reviews, reinvestment, and diversification.

To prepare for the future of passive income, stay connected to the DeFi community. Join governance forums, read protocol updates, and test new tools with small amounts. Subscribe to yield aggregators and DeFi newsletters. The next generation of crypto income won't be about chasing hype. It will be about building smart, efficient systems that grow with minimal effort and maximal protection.

As we move into the final chapter, we'll summarize everything you've learned—showing how to put all the pieces together into a complete, sustainable crypto income plan designed for long-term wealth and freedom.

Xavier's Leap Into the Future of Crypto Income

Xavier had always been ahead of the curve. As a former fintech analyst turned crypto educator, he wasn't just interested in where DeFi was—he was obsessed with where it was going. While others were chasing short-term yield farms and hype tokens, Xavier was quietly building a future-proof income system powered by the latest innovations in blockchain finance. His friends called him overly cautious, but they didn't see what he saw: a tidal wave of opportunity through liquid staking, tokenized real-world assets, and AI-driven yield automation.

It all started when Xavier realized his Ethereum staking rewards were sitting idle. He had ETH staked in Lido, earning 4%, but he hadn't touched his stETH. Then he discovered he could use that stETH as collateral in Aave, or stake it again in Curve's stETH/ETH pool to earn even more. Suddenly, a single yield stream became two. And then three. Xavier had unlocked the first layer of the future: **liquid staking derivatives**—yield-bearing assets that could travel across DeFi.

From there, his curiosity led him to **real-world asset (RWA) tokens**. He discovered Ondo Finance, where he could buy tokenized U.S. treasury bill exposure and earn a consistent 5% yield without touching volatile crypto assets. It was mind-blowing. He was earning stable, regulated income inside a DeFi wallet—with no bank in sight. Soon, he diversified into Maple Finance for tokenized business loans and Goldfinch for community-based lending. His portfolio, once 100% digital, now included yield from **real-world economies**, all accessible with a few clicks.

But Xavier didn't stop there. He became an early tester of AI-powered DeFi platforms. One app connected to his wallet and, after a few prompts, recommended where to deploy idle USDC based on current rates, gas fees, and security scores. Another let him schedule actions like "harvest and restake every Sunday" or "move funds if APY drops below 7%." What once took him hours of manual checking was now handled by smart contracts and machine logic. It wasn't just passive income—it was **autonomous income**.

Xavier also embraced the **cross-chain revolution**. He no longer limited himself to Ethereum. Instead, he farmed stablecoins on Arbitrum, lent on Avalanche, staked on Cosmos, and managed everything from a single wallet with multi-chain visibility. He used LayerZero to bridge assets seamlessly and even set up rules to auto-rotate capital to the best-performing chain each month. His income streams were no longer dependent on one ecosystem. They flowed like a river across protocols, layers, and networks.

Eventually, Xavier noticed another trend: **crypto income tools were becoming embedded in everything**. His wallet suggested staking options with a single tap. His DEX offered auto-compounding strategies. Even fintech apps were beginning to support crypto-native yield products. The barriers were dropping—and soon, he knew, millions of people would be earning passive income without ever realizing they were interacting with DeFi.

Still, Xavier remained disciplined. He continued using insurance on high-value positions, tracking everything in DeBank, and setting quarterly goals. He updated his portfolio tracker to include liquid staking positions, RWA-backed tokens, and AI-assisted vaults. And when markets dipped or narratives shifted, his income held steady—not because he was lucky, but because he had built something that **wasn't reliant on hype**.

Today, Xavier earns more from his crypto income system than he ever did in his corporate role. He teaches others how to prepare for the coming wave of innovation, helping them understand that the real opportunity isn't just in new coins—but in new systems. Systems that earn while you sleep. Systems that don't break when the market turns. Systems that adapt and evolve automatically.

He tells his students, “If you build your crypto income like a business—diversified, automated, and future-ready—you’ll never need to chase another trend again.”

Chapter 10: Putting It All Together, Your Crypto Income Blueprint

You've now explored staking, yield farming, lending, vault automation, risk management, and the future of crypto income. The next step is integration—bringing everything together into a complete, sustainable, and scalable crypto passive income plan. This final chapter serves as your **blueprint**: a step-by-step system to create consistent, diversified cash flow that adapts to your financial goals, risk profile, and time availability.

Start by defining your **income target**. Be specific. How much crypto income do you want per month—and by when? For example, if your target is $1,000/month in passive income at an average yield of 15%, you'll need about $80,000 deployed efficiently. If you start with $10,000 and reinvest 100% of the income monthly, you can use compounding to close that gap over time. Once you've defined your goal, reverse-engineer your strategy using the core yield methods.

Break your capital into **core allocation buckets**:

- **40–50% to stablecoin lending** (e.g., USDC, DAI on Aave, Compound, Curve): stable, predictable, low-risk income.

- **25–35% to staking** (e.g., ETH, ADA, DOT via Lido, Rocket Pool, or native wallets): long-term network security yield.

- **15–25% to yield farming** (preferably in blue-chip or stablecoin pools): higher potential returns with managed risk.

- **Optional 5–10% to experimental strategies**: liquid staking, RWAs, new vaults, or AI-automated DeFi tools.

Use **risk-adjusted portfolio design**. Consider each strategy's volatility, smart contract risk, liquidity, and token behavior. Assign each strategy a risk score (1–5) and cap exposure based on your personal comfort zone. If you're risk-averse, shift weight toward lending and staking. If you're risk-tolerant and active, increase exposure to vaults and farms with safety checks in place.

Now establish your **tracking and review system**:

- Use dashboards like **Zapper, DeBank, or APY.Vision** to monitor real-time performance.

- Create a monthly **review ritual**: harvest rewards, update your tracker, and calculate net yield.

- Use spreadsheets or Notion to track deposits, earnings, gas fees, vault APYs, and capital rotations.

Build in **automation where possible**:

- Use platforms like **Beefy, Yearn, or Reaper** to automate compounding.
- Explore **DeFi Saver or Instadapp** to create harvesting and reallocation rules.
- Use **Revoke.cash** and a hardware wallet to maintain strong wallet hygiene.

Create a **cash-out strategy** to convert your crypto income into usable funds:

- Use stablecoins to transfer to fiat via centralized exchanges or crypto debit cards.
- Set monthly or quarterly cash-out percentages to cover living expenses or reinvest into real-world assets.
- Keep a safety buffer in stablecoins for emergencies or rebalancing needs.

Layer in **protection strategies**:

- Use **insurance protocols** for high-value vaults or critical staking positions.
- Keep all long-term holdings in **hardware wallets**, and split capital across chains.
- Document your seed phrases and DeFi instructions in a clear, offline plan for family or partners.

Stay **informed but not overwhelmed**. Subscribe to one or two trusted newsletters like DeFi Llama, The Defiant, or Bankless. Join a few focused Discord or Telegram communities. Set rules for yourself: test new strategies with no more than 1% of your portfolio at first. Don't let constant noise derail your long-term approach.

Finally, revisit your **income system quarterly**. Ask:

- Which platforms are overperforming or underperforming?
- Has my income increased or decreased in the past 90 days?
- Are there new yield opportunities worth reallocating into?

- Is my allocation still in line with my risk tolerance and time commitment?

Crypto income is not a static system—it's a living strategy. It evolves as technology, markets, and your goals change. But with structure, discipline, and automation, you can make it consistent, reliable, and powerful.

The passive income revolution has already begun. And now, you're ready to lead it—not by guessing, but by building a system that works for you. Whether your goal is financial independence, side income, or just making your money work harder—crypto offers the tools, and you now have the blueprint.

Priya's Complete Crypto Income System

Priya never saw herself as an investor. She was a school teacher by trade, meticulous and patient, but cautious when it came to money. For years, she'd relied on traditional savings accounts, low-yield CDs, and a conservative retirement plan. But everything changed during the pandemic. She started exploring alternative income strategies online, and soon stumbled across the idea of earning **passive income with crypto**. One article became ten. Ten videos turned into a rabbit hole. And before long, Priya made the decision to try something new—not wild, not risky, but structured.

She didn't start with thousands of dollars or complex strategies. She started with a single goal: **earn $200 per month** passively within one year. With her savings and part of her bonus, she allocated $10,000 and built a plan.

Her first step was to **define the structure**. She divided her portfolio into three categories:

- **Stablecoin lending** on Aave and Compound, for about 45% of her capital.
- **Staking** ETH through Lido and ADA through Yoroi, about 30%.
- **Yield farming** with auto-compounding vaults on Beefy Finance, using stablecoin pairs for minimal risk, about 20%. She kept the final 5% as an "experiment fund" for new opportunities or testing ideas from trusted DeFi newsletters.

Next, she **set up her tracking system**. A color-coded spreadsheet listed all her positions, amounts, platforms, chains, and yields. She reviewed it each Sunday after breakfast—her new version of financial self-care. She started using **Zapper** and **DeBank** to monitor her holdings, and made it a habit to harvest and restake monthly to keep the system compounding.

Over time, she added **automation**. She deposited funds into vaults that auto-compounded and began using tools like **Revoke.cash** to manage permissions. She installed a Ledger wallet for long-term safety and took the time to write a simple document for her sister explaining how to access her assets in case something happened.

By month six, her system was producing $90/month. It wasn't enough to change her life—but it was enough to notice. That $90 covered groceries for a week, her phone bill, or gas. The best part? It worked **while she was teaching, traveling, or sleeping**. There were no charts to read. No trades to make. Her crypto worked for her—not the other way around.

When markets dipped, Priya stayed calm. Her lending and staking continued paying. Her farming positions adjusted as she rebalanced. She didn't chase trends or hop from one protocol to the next. She stuck to her plan, reallocated based on performance, and reinvested most of her rewards.

By the end of the year, she hit her goal: $212 in monthly crypto income.

But it was more than the money. Priya had built confidence. She understood how decentralized finance worked. She could explain staking and lending to anyone. She even began mentoring a few coworkers who were curious about crypto but terrified by the volatility. She taught them what she had done: start small, stay diversified, automate what you can, and protect everything.

Now, Priya is working on her next goal: **$500/month in 18 months**, and eventually, $1,000/month. She still teaches full-time, but with a lighter heart—knowing that in the background, she's building something that's growing every day.

Her system isn't fancy or complicated. But it's **complete**. It's her version of financial freedom. And she built it—just like you can—one smart step at a time.

Welcome to the future of wealth

As we close this book, it's clear that we're living in a financial revolution. The ability to earn passive income through crypto was unthinkable a decade ago—but today, it's not only possible, it's practical, scalable, and accessible to anyone with a wallet and a plan. Whether you're a complete beginner or a savvy investor, the crypto economy is offering a new kind of freedom—one not tied to banks, borders, or bosses.

Throughout this journey, we've explored staking, yield farming, lending, and automation. We've shown how to diversify, protect, reinvest, and adapt your income strategy. You've learned that crypto income is not about luck or hype—it's about systems, consistency, and long-term thinking. It rewards those who are intentional, curious, and cautious.

We've met people like Lisa, Malik, Olivia, and Priya—everyday individuals who took control of their financial destiny using DeFi tools. They didn't need massive wealth, technical degrees, or insider access. They just needed a starting point, a structured plan, and the courage to take the first step. Their stories are real—and so is the income they now receive every week, every month, on autopilot.

You now have the complete framework. You've seen how to break your income goals into realistic numbers, how to choose platforms with confidence, and how to build a risk-managed portfolio. Most importantly, you've learned how to protect your earnings, automate your workflow, and scale your results—so that every dollar you earn today multiplies tomorrow.

The world is changing fast. AI is integrating with DeFi. Real-world assets are coming on-chain. Regulation is becoming clearer. Wallets are becoming smarter. If you keep learning, keep testing, and keep building your system with intention—you won't just keep up. You'll thrive.

Start small if you need to. Test. Track. Adjust. Then grow. This is your time to build freedom—not through more hours, but through smarter tools. The crypto economy runs 24/7. Your income can too.

And always remember: you don't need to trade coins to profit. You just need a well-designed system that works while you sleep.

Welcome to the future of wealth. You're already part of it.

www.ingramcontent.com/pod-product-compliance
Lightning Source LLC
LaVergne TN
LVHW022013200926
848481LV00007B/2377
9798349644559